My Flashback 70th Birthday Quiz Book

Turning 70 Humor for People Born in the '50s

by JEST FEST

The INNARDS

PART 1 – CHILDHOOD

Things Only '50s Kids Will Remember

Toon Anagrams
Toy Number Puzzle Picture
Movie Search
Sweet Sudoku
Cool Crossword

PART 2 – TEENHOOD

Things Only '60s Teens Will Remember

Complete the Lyrics
Groovy Crossword
The Odd Couple
Fave Gadget Maze
Pastime NPP
Name the Movie
Past Price Is Right

PART 3 – The ANSWERS

BONUS

MORE FROM JEST FEST

This paperback edition first published
in 2020 by Dialog Abroad Books.

Copyright © Jest Fest, 2020.

2   4   6   8   10   9   7   5   3   1

ISBN: 978-3-948706-58-6

PART 1: CHILDHOOD

Things Only '50s Kids Will Remember

A ton of cool stuff debuted in the '50s and '50s kids were the first generation to enjoy them.

But even though you lived through it, it's easy to forget all the things that made the '50s truly unique.

So, get your pen ready for nostalgia-filled puzzles that will bring back your childhood memories from the '50s!

Toon Anagrams

Rearrange these phrases to reveal the names of some great cartoon characters you loved growing up in the '50s.

Dewy Odor Cowpoke

Answer: _____

My Eight Sumo

Answer: _____

Ken Jelled A Check

Answer: _____

Toy Number Puzzle Picture

In any order you wish, copy the contents of each square in the jumbled picture below to the same numbered square in the blank grid on the next page until the entire puzzle is done, then add vivid '50s shades to your masterpiece.

What cool 1950s toy is depicted here?

_____

0	1	2	3	4	5	6	7
8	9	10	11	12	13	14	15
16	17	18	19	20	21	22	23
24	25	26	27	28	29	30	31
32	33	34	35	36	37	38	39
40	41	42	43	44	45	46	47
48	49	50	51	52	53	54	55
56	57	58	59	60	61	62	63

Movie Search

The titles of four kids' movies from the '50s that defined your childhood are hidden below. Can you find and circle them?

```
S  L  E  E  P  I  N  G  B  E  A  S  T  Y
S  L  E  E  P  I  N  G  B  E  A  S  T  Y
S  L  E  A  P  I  N  G  B  E  A  T  T  Y
S  L  E  E  L  I  N  G  B  E  A  R  T  Y
S  L  E  E  P  L  N  G  B  E  A  E  T  Y
S  L  E  E  P  I  E  G  B  E  A  A  T  Y
S  L  E  E  P  I  N  R  B  R  A  S  T  Y
S  L  E  E  P  I  N  G  E  E  A  U  T  Y
S  L  E  E  P  I  N  L  B  D  A  R  T  Y
S  L  E  E  P  I  L  G  B  E  N  E  T  Y
S  L  E  E  P  E  N  G  B  E  A  I  T  Y
S  L  E  E  Y  I  N  G  B  E  A  S  C  Y
S  L  E  D  P  I  N  G  B  E  A  L  T  Y
S  L  L  E  P  I  N  G  B  E  A  A  T  Y
S  O  E  E  P  E  T  E  R  P  A  N  T  Y
S  L  E  E  P  I  N  G  B  E  A  D  T  Y
```

Sweet Sudoku

Fill in the blank squares so that each row, each column and each 3-by-3 block contain the letters A, E, I, P, R, T, U, X, Z.

The word you produce from the highlighted squares completes the following phrase to describe you:

"AS A 1950s KID, I LOVED EATING _____"

E	U	R				I		T
			E				Z	U
	X		U	T	I			
R	E					Z		
	Z	U	A		T	P	X	
		T					A	E
			I	A	U	T	E	P
T	I				R			
U		P				R		X

Cool Crossword

Test your knowledge of popular children's toys, books, breakfast cereals, and drinks from the '50s.

1. A plastic model of a vegetable that you decorated with a variety of plastic body parts.
2. A book by Dr. Seuss about an elephant who can perceive sound from an unusual source.
3. A chocolate-flavored puffed grain breakfast cereal eaten by Sonny the Cuckoo Bird.
4. An artificially flavored drink mix engineered to taste like orange without any of the vitamins or minerals.
5. A book about an eccentric stranger who visits two children home alone and having a very dull day.
6. A modeling compound you loved to play with until you heard an angry voice say, "Don't mix the colors!".
7. The nickname for Tony's sugar-coated corn flakes.
8. Nestlé's powdered drink mix to make chocolate-flavored milkshakes at home.
9. A flavored drink mix advertised by a red, anthropomorphic pitcher.
10. A book about a pig named Wilbur and his friendship with a barn spider.
11. The original name of Dig'em Frog's sweetened puffed wheat breakfast cereal that's now called "Honey _____".

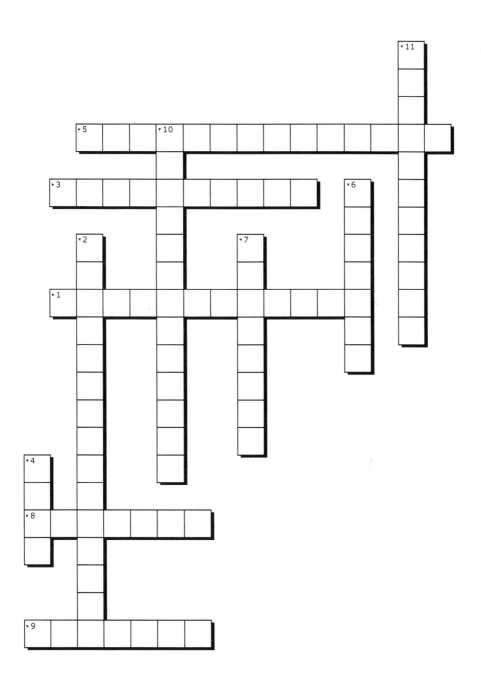

PART 2: TEENHOOD

Things Only '60s Teens Will Remember

Although everything changes when you become a teenager no matter when and where you were born, the world in the '60s was a very different place than it is today.

We all know you enjoyed plenty of the usual coming-of-age experiences on your journey to adulthood (often before legal age!). But when the calendar switched to the year 1960, your taste in clothes, hairstyles, and music all changed.

With pen still in hand, it's time to see how well you remember the groovy stuff that defined your 1960s adolescence.

Complete the Lyrics

Nobody writes songs like they did in the '60s. Fill in the blanks below with the correct lyrics and prove yourself a '60s music expert.

"Oh _____, say to me

You'll let me be your _____

And please, say to me

You'll let me _____ your _____"

"Then I saw her _____, now I'm a _____

Not a _____, of doubt in my mind

I'm in love, and I'm a _____

I couldn't _____ her if I tried"

"Yeah, you should see my little _____

You should see my, my little _____

She really knows how to _____

She knows how to _____"

Groovy Crossword

Test your knowledge of iconic fashion trends, hairstyles, magazines, and dance crazes from the '60s.

1. A hairstyle that created quite a "buzz" due to its resemblance to the distinctive nose of a B-52 Bomber.

2. A style of women's fashion boot that Nancy said were "made for walkin'".

3. A dance singer Little Eva told everyone to "do" down by the railroad.

4. A style of trousers that seemed more suited to a child than Audrey Hepburn.

5. A dance move useful for squishing root vegetables that Dee Dee said it was time for.

6. A magazine with celebrity stories, posters, and trivia similar to Teen B____ and aimed at teen girls.

7. A "dreamy" dance where you lift your right arm and leg, then lift your left arm and leg. Sounds simple, but at high speeds, it can result in craziness.

8. A short yet dramatic hairstyle that was the ultimate act of rebellion. Just ask Twiggy and Brigitte Bardot.

9. A style of pants that become wider from the knees downward, forming a bell-like shape of the trouser leg.

10. A short, bowl-shaped, shaggy hairstyle for men that looked fitting for cleaning the kitchen floor.

Across:
4. CAPRIPANTS
1. THEBEEHIVE
5. THEMASHEDPOTATO
10. THEMOPTOP
2. GOGOBOOTS

Down:
3. THELOCOMOTION
7. THEFREDDIE
6. TIGERBEAT
9. BELLBOTTOMS
8. MODBOB

The Odd Couple

These celebrities got hitched in the '60s, but which couple didn't get the happily ever after they were hoping for and split before the decade's end?

Elvis & Priscilla

Frank & Mia

Johnny & June

Fave Gadget Maze

What a great decade for technology! Quickly and without thinking, select and trace a dotted line A, B or C along the path to reveal what your subconscious thinks was the best gadget of the '60s.

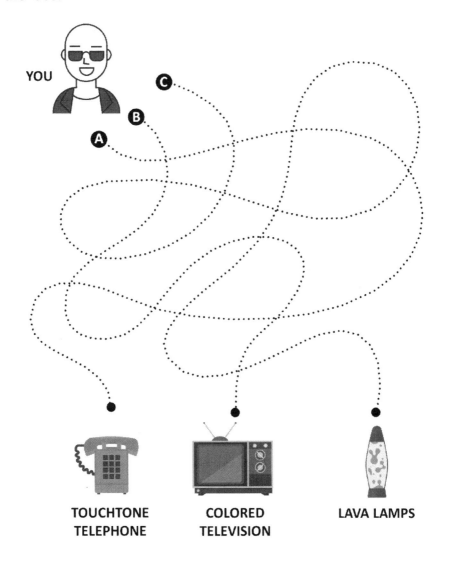

TOUCHTONE TELEPHONE

COLORED TELEVISION

LAVA LAMPS

Pastime NPP

In any order you wish, copy the contents of each square in the jumbled picture below to the same numbered square in the blank grid on the next page until the entire puzzle is done, then add vivid '60s shades to your masterpiece.

0	1	2	3	4	5	6	7
8	9	10	11	12	13	14	15
16	17	18	19	20	21	22	23
24	25	26	27	28	29	30	31
32	33	34	35	36	37	38	39
40	41	42	43	44	45	46	47
48	49	50	51	52	53	54	55
56	57	58	59	60	61	62	63

Name the Movie

Guess the classic movies that '60s teens adored from these legendary quotes.

"Frankie: You know, the only thing I've
studied this semester is you.
Dolores: Well, I hope you don't flunk.   _____
Frankie: Well, there's always summer
school, you know."

"Girls like me weren't built to be
educated. We were made to have
children. That's my ambition - to be a   _____
walking, talking baby factory."

"No, dear not a kook - a Martian."   _____

"In dealing with women, a man must
shun reason and logic."   _____

"Honey, you know I never go out with a
married man on the first date."   _____

"Susan Evers: Switch places!
Sharon McKendrick: Switch?"   _____

"Merrie: I was big enough before!"   _____

"'Pookie' Adams: Some people guzzle God
like He was a keg of beer."   _____

"There hasn't been so much excitement
around here since Tony Curtis came in
for a checkup."   _____

"Senator, I'm sure my son has a very
good reason for paralyzing the country." _____

Past Price Is Right

The cost of stuff has skyrocketed in recent times. But can you guess how much these young adult essentials cost in the '60s?

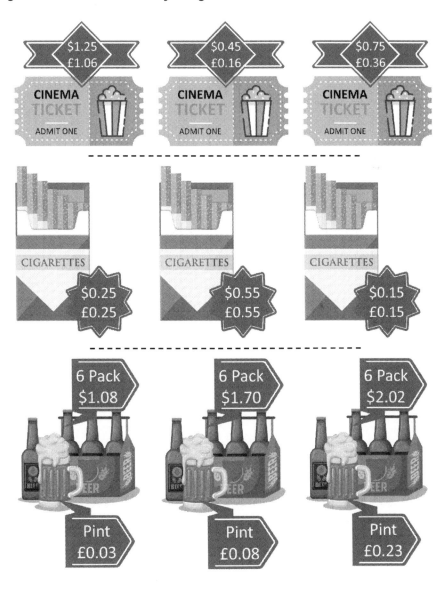

PART 3: The ANSWERS

Toon Anagrams

Rearrange these phrases to reveal some great cartoons you probably watched growing up in the '50s.

Dewy Odor Cowpoke

Answer: <u>Woody Woodpecker</u>

My Eight Sumo

Answer: <u>Mighty Mouse</u>

Ken Jelled A Check

Answer: <u>Heckle and Jeckle</u>

Toy Number Puzzle Picture

In any order you wish, copy the contents of each square in the jumbled picture below to the same numbered square in the blank grid on the next page until the entire puzzle is done, then add vivid '50s shades to your masterpiece.

What cool 1950s toy is depicted here?

<u>View Master</u>

Movie Search

The titles of four kids' movies from the '50s that defined your childhood are hidden below. Can you find and circle them?

```
S  L  E  E  P  I  N  G  B  E  A  S  T  Y
S  L  E  E  P  I  N  G  B  E  A  S  T  Y
S  L  E  A  P  I  N  G  B  E  A  T  T  Y
S  L  E  E  L  I  N  G  B  E  A  R  T  Y
S  L  E  E  P  L  N  G  B  E  A  E  T  Y
S  L  E  E  P  I  E  G  B  E  A  A  T  Y
S  L  E  E  P  I  N  R  B  R  A  S  T  Y
S  L  E  E  P  I  N  G  E  E  A  U  T  Y
S  L  E  E  P  I  N  L  B  D  A  R  T  Y
S  L  E  E  P  I  L  G  B  E  N  E  T  Y
S  L  E  E  P  E  N  G  B  E  A  I  T  Y
S  L  E  E  Y  I  N  G  B  E  A  S  C  Y
S  L  E  D  P  I  N  G  B  E  A  L  T  Y
S  L  L  E  P  I  N  G  B  E  A  A  T  Y
S  O  E  E  P  E  T  E  R  P  A  N  T  Y
S  L  E  E  P  I  N  G  B  E  A  D  T  Y
```

Sweet Sudoku

Fill in the blank squares so that each row, each column and each 3-by-3 block contain the letters A, E, I, P, R, T, U, X, Z.

The word you produce from the highlighted squares completes the following phrase to describe you:

"AS A 1950s KID, I LOVED EATING PEZ"

E	U	R	Z	X	A	I	P	T
A	T	I	E	R	P	X	Z	U
P	X	Z	U	T	I	E	R	A
R	E	A	P	U	X	Z	T	I
I	Z	U	A	E	T	P	X	R
X	P	T	R	I	Z	U	A	E
Z	R	X	I	A	U	T	E	P
T	I	E	X	P	R	A	U	Z
U	A	P	T	Z	E	R	I	X

Cool Crossword

Test your knowledge of popular children's toys, books, breakfast cereals, and drinks from the '50s.

1. A plastic model of a vegetable that you decorated with a variety of plastic body parts.
2. A book by Dr. Seuss about an elephant who can perceive sound from an unusual source.
3. A chocolate-flavored puffed grain breakfast cereal eaten by Sonny the Cuckoo Bird.
4. An artificially flavored drink mix engineered to taste like orange without any of the vitamins or minerals.
5. A book about an eccentric stranger who visits two children home alone and having a very dull day.
6. A modeling compound you loved to play with until you heard an angry voice say, "Don't mix the colors!".
7. The nickname for Tony's sugar-coated corn flakes.
8. Nestlé's powdered drink mix to make chocolate-flavored milkshakes at home.
9. A flavored drink mix advertised by a red, anthropomorphic pitcher.
10. A book about a pig named Wilbur and his friendship with a barn spider.
11. The original name of Dig'em Frog's sweetened puffed wheat breakfast cereal that's now called "Honey _____".

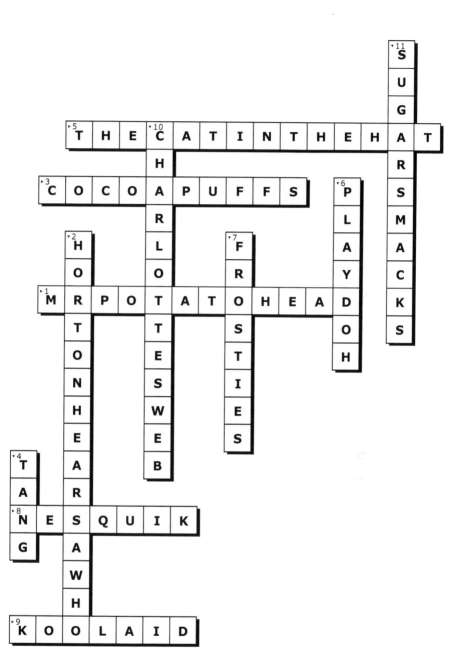

Complete the Lyrics

Nobody writes songs like they did in the '60s. Fill in the blanks below with the correct lyrics and prove yourself a '60s music expert.

"Oh <u>please</u>, say to me
You'll let me be your <u>man</u>
And please, say to me
You'll let me <u>hold</u> your <u>hand</u>"

"Then I saw her <u>face</u>, now I'm a <u>believer</u>
Not a <u>trace</u>, of doubt in my mind
I'm in love, and I'm a <u>believer</u>
I couldn't <u>leave</u> her if I tried"

"Yeah, you should see my little <u>sis</u>
You should see my, my little <u>sis</u>
She really knows how to <u>rock</u>
She knows how to <u>twist</u>"

The Odd Couple

These celebrities got hitched in the '60s, but which couple didn't get the happily ever after they were hoping for and split before the decade's end?

Groovy Crossword

Test your knowledge of iconic fashion trends, hairstyles, magazines, and dance crazes from the '60s.

1. A hairstyle that created quite a "buzz" due to its resemblance to the distinctive nose of a B-52 Bomber.
2. A style of women's fashion boot that Nancy said were "made for walkin'".
3. A dance singer Little Eva told everyone to "do" down by the railroad.
4. A style of trousers that seemed more suited to a child than Audrey Hepburn.
5. A dance move useful for squishing root vegetables that Dee Dee said it was time for.
6. A magazine with celebrity stories, posters, and trivia similar to Teen B___ and aimed at teen girls.
7. A "dreamy" dance where you lift your right arm and leg, then lift your left arm and leg. Sounds simple, but at high speeds, it can result in craziness.
8. A short yet dramatic hairstyle that was the ultimate act of rebellion. Just ask Twiggy and Brigitte Bardot.
9. A style of pants that become wider from the knees downward, forming a bell-like shape of the trouser leg.
10. A short, bowl-shaped, shaggy hairstyle for men that looked fitting for cleaning the kitchen floor.

Pastime NPP

In any order you wish, copy the contents of each square in the jumbled picture below to the same numbered square in the blank grid on the next page until the entire puzzle is done, then add vivid '60s shades to your masterpiece.

Name the Movie

Guess the classic movies that '60s teens adored from these legendary quotes.

"Frankie: You know, the only thing I've studied this semester is you.
Dolores: Well, I hope you don't flunk.
Frankie: Well, there's always summer school, you know."
Beach Party

"Girls like me weren't built to be educated. We were made to have children. That's my ambition - to be a walking, talking baby factory."
Where the Boys Are

"No, dear not a kook - a Martian."
Pajama Party

"In dealing with women, a man must shun reason and logic."
Billie

"Honey, you know I never go out with a married man on the first date."
Lord Love a Duck

"Susan Evers: Switch places!
Sharon McKendrick: Switch?"
The Parent Trap

"Merrie: I was big enough before!"
Village of the Giants

"'Pookie' Adams: Some people guzzle God like He was a keg of beer."
The Sterile Cuckoo

"There hasn't been so much excitement around here since Tony Curtis came in for a checkup."
Tammy and the Doctor

"Senator, I'm sure my son has a very good reason for paralyzing the country."
Wild in the Streets

Past Price Is Right

The cost of stuff has skyrocketed in recent times. But can you guess how much these young adult essentials cost in the '60s?

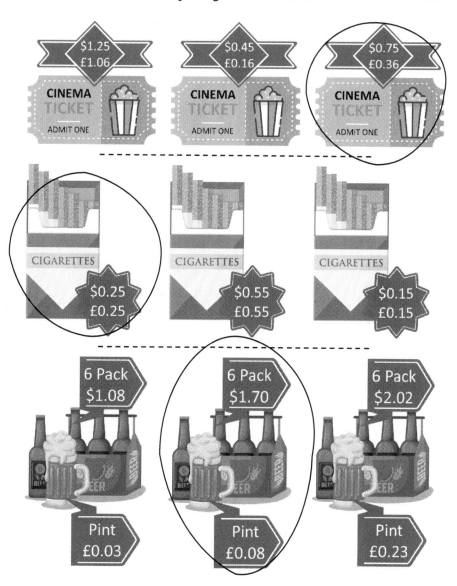

| $1.25 £1.06 | $0.45 £0.16 | $0.75 £0.36 |

CINEMA TICKET — ADMIT ONE

| CIGARETTES $0.25 £0.25 | CIGARETTES $0.55 £0.55 | CIGARETTES $0.15 £0.15 |

| 6 Pack $1.08 | 6 Pack $1.70 | 6 Pack $2.02 |
| Pint £0.03 | Pint £0.08 | Pint £0.23 |

BONUS: Badge

To make your milestone birthday even more special, here is an exclusive and exquisite badge for you to cut out and wear with PRIDE.

Go on... let everyone know just how grateful you were to be a '50s kid!

More From JEST FEST

Did you enjoy your journey back through simpler times? I hope it brought back many happy memories and made you laugh.

If you want more giggle-inspiring books to lighten the mood, I've got you covered.

(Female version also available)

Printed in Great Britain
by Amazon

83950845R00029